NARRATIVE

OF THE LIFE OF

PAUL CUFFE,

A descendant of an Indian family, which formerly resided in the eastern part of Connecticut and constituted a part of that fierce and warlike tribe of Indians called Pequots, of whose exploits in the early Wars of New-England, the reader may become acquainted by perusing "Trumbull's History of the Indian Wars."

THE subject of this narrative was born in the town of Westport, in the State of Massachusetts. His father, Paul Cuffe, was a sea-faring man, and had the command of a number of merchant vessels. It was with him that I made my first voyage, when a boy twelve years old. This was in the year 1808. On the morning of a pleasant day in the month of May, of that year, we hoisted sail and stood out for sea. There were 16 hands on board. This was new business to me, and with the novelty attending a sea voyage I was highly pleased. Nothing uncommon attended this voyage, which was made to Passamaquaddy, for Plaster of Paris. We made this voyage down in about 10 days. After loading our vessel. which took two weeks, we again set sail for Wilmington, in Delaware, at which port we safely arrived in 16 days, discharged our freight, took in ballast and 300 bushels of apples, and sailed for Savannah, in Georgia, where we arrived without any accident to mar the pleasure of the voyage, in about twenty days, where we again discharged our freight and reloaded our vessel with Cotton,

Rice and Logwood. Here we lay three months in making preparation for sea again. From this place we made out into the broad Atlantic with all sails fluttering in the balmy breeze, and all hands full of hope and buoyant with expectation. This was a long, tedious voyage, as the reader will readily imagine when I inform him that we sailed a great number of days in a north-ward direction, until we made the Grand Banks: then we steered away for the northern coast of Scotland, which we reached in about fifty days. Thence we continued our course around the Orknies into the Northern Sea, and made the entrance to the Baltic through what is called the Sleeve; thence along the coast of Copenhagen northward to Gottenburgh, a flourishing town in West Gothland in Sweden. Here we lay six weeks, sold our lading, and took in a load of iron, steel and hemp. From thence we sailed for Elsinore, a seaport of Denmark, where we took in a number of passengers for Philadelphia, at which place we arrived after a long passage, somtime in the month of September, 1809. During this voyage we had much rough weather; so much so, that we were compelled to throw overboard fifty tons of iron while on the Grand Banks. During this gale we lost our fore-top-mast, jib-boom and long boat.

At this port we sold our load; after which my father put me to a high school in Williams' Alley, where I remained two years. This was an excellent school, taught by a Friend Quaker, a very worthy man. whom I shall ever have cause to respect for his many acts of kindness towards me.

After the close of my term at school, I returned home to Westport, after an absence of three years and five months. If the reader has ever been a long while absent from home, he can easily imagine my feelings on my arrival at the dear paternal mansion Here I again saw my father and mother, brothers and sisters, where I remained but three weeks before I again left the fire side of my dear parents to launch out upon the broad Atlantic's briny bosom. At the expiration of the above term, I shipped aboard of the brig Traveller, Capt. Thomas Warner, for Kennebec, state of Maine. On our passage to this place, our vessel capsized about 10 o'clock at night, which caused us much trouble to get her righted again; but after four hours' struggle, and by the aid of our Great Father, we got the ship to rights, and went on our passage, which we finished in about seven days from this event. Here we sold our loading and took in a load of pine lumber. At this place we were detained but about ten days, when we again hoisted sail for Westport, where we arrived in ten days thereafter. Here I tarried with my family but four weeks before I again shipped aboard of the last named vessel for Lisbon, in Portugal, where we arrived after a rough passage of forty-five days. Our lading was 525 barrels of whale oil, which we sold at Lisbon. While at this place we heard the roar of the cannon in an engagement between a division of the army of the Great Napoleon and the English and Portuguese troops, and the night after this battle the writer saw five hundred wounded soldiers brought into Lisbon to have their wounds dressed. In this engagement the English and Portuguese repelled the army of Napoleon, and caused them to fall back a number of miles.

Here we tarried about four months, and took in one hundred and eighty merino sheep, being the second load ever taken to the United States. Besides these we took in Salt and Wine. Our passage back to Westport was made in thirty-five days. Here we tarried but one week, and again after taking in ballast, proceeded to sea, and steered away for Edenton, North Carolina; at which port we arrived in 16 days. Here we were detained about six weeks. After loading our brig with shingles and herring, we again stood out for sea, and made for St Domingo, an Island of the West Indies, peopled by free blacks, having a republican form of government.

During this passage we encountered heavy gales of wind, and came very near being shipwrecked, but we were all preserved, and in 16 days from the time we set sail, we made Port Au Prince. This is a large sea port town, situated between two high mountains. This place is the residence of the chief magistrate of the nation. Robert Boyer was then clothed with the presidential power This personage was of commanding aspect, and appeared to be a mulatto. He used every day to call out his body guard, who were a fine looking set of fellows as I had ever seen. They appeared to understand military tactics to perfection. They were elegantly dressed in red frocks and trowsers, faced with blue and green. On the whole, they might be called first rate. soldiers. Boyer was most superbly dressed and equipped, and on horseback made an elegant appearance.

This is an unhealthy place for strangers, our crew being mostly sick while there. We stopped at this place about three weeks, during which time we took in a cargo of Coffee and Sugar. From this port we sailed sometime in October 1812. At this time the government of my native country and Great Britain were at war. During this voyage, which was made to New-York, we were chased by a British man-of-war for more than four hours, while off Bermuda; but we out-sailed her and made our escape. When off Cape Hatteras, we lost our fore top-sail during a heavy squall of wind. We reached the quarantine at New-York, after a passage of 13 days. Here we had to lay to for 3 days, for the purpose of being examined by the health officer; after which we went up to the city, where we discharged our freight which took about one week, when we again sailed for Westport, the place of my nativity. Here I saw my father and mother, with whom I stayed but 5 weeks before I again left my peaceful home and all the many little endearments which always surround the paternal mansion, for New Bedford, a sea port town in the south-eastern part of Massachusetts, where I shipped aboard the Atlas, a whaleman, bound to the Brazil banks. We hoisted sail just at night, and steered away in an east northeast direction until we crossed the Grand banks, and then stood away for the Azores, where, after 20 days' sail, we made the Island of Carvo, one of that group of Islands. Here we stopped a few days and took in 500 bushels of potatoes and 100 bushels of onions. There was no harbor in this place; so we were obliged to go ashore in our boats. The people brought down the above articles on their backs. Men, women and children were all engaged in supplying us with the above articles. We paid them in oil, of which they were very fond. What they do with it I know not. They were a very kind people to strangers, but poor. From this place we sailed for the Cape De Verds, on the coast of Africa. We were forty-two days in sailing from the former to the latter island. We touched at the island of Buenavista, one of this group, where we took in thirty-two hogs, for which we paid corn, meal and bread. These people are of a very dark hue, and speak the Potuguese language. Here we stopped but four days, when we set all sails and steered away a southwest course, for the Brazil Banks, where we arrived, after a sail of forty-two days.

Here we commenced fishing for whale, but for a time had bad luck, owing to the drunken habits of our Captain. We sunk twelve whales before we caught one. Then we caught six in the course of two weeks. I harpooned all these, and assisted in taking and towing them along side the ship. After we get a whale along side, we hitch our blubber hooks into the head, after severing it from the body, then, with our windlass, draw it aboard, and dip the oil out, which sometimes amounts to more than fifty barrels. After this we, commence cutting the whale in a circular manner with our spades; then we hitch the blubber hooks into the commencement next to where the head was taken off, and by pulling at the windlass, take off a large piece which will usually when tried and strained, produce ten barrels of oil. Before heaving on board this piece, another hook is fastened below the one to be taken off; when this is done with a cross blow from the spade, the first piece is separated from the rest of the whale. Then the cutting is continued in the same manner as before mentioned, and another piece torn off and swung aboard. This operation keeps the whale constantly rolling over until the mass of flesh is stripped from the carcass, which is then permitted to float off, or sink, and it becomes the sport of sharks, who feed upon the little flesh which remains after it has gone through the hands of the whalemen.

Here we stayed but six weeks before we took in 1600 barrels of oil. This was about 300 miles off the Brazil coast.—From this place we set sail with our cargo about the middle of June 1813, for New Bedford, where we arrived in fifty-seven days. When off Block Island we saw the keel of a brig, upon which were marked the names of a number of persons who undoubtedly belonged to her and had died upon the wreck.

We were about five days unloading ship, after which the hands were paid off and discharged. After this I went again to visit my parents at Westport, where I stayed but two weeks before I went to Philadelphia across land, and shipped aboard the Dorothea, a Letter of Marque brig, Captain Aaron Pitney, bound to St. Jago, loaded with flour and hoop-poles. This brig mounted ten guns. When out two days we fell in with an English brig of ten guns, to which we gave chase, and fought her for about two hours, when she got away from us, we being unable to gain upon her in consequence of having our rigging badly cut to pieces. In this action we lost two men killed and the Captain badly wounded.

About three days after the above action, about 4 o'clock A. M., we discovered an English frigate, which gave chase to us, and fired several guns, none of which reached us. This vessel we outsailed and left far behind by 2 o'clock P. M. Eight days after this chase, we reached St. Jago, and discharged our freight. Here we tarried three weeks and sold the brig to a Spanish gentleman. We then took passage in the American schooner Mary, bound to Alexandria, in the District of Columbia, upon the river Thames. This vessel had been trading under an English license, and had been taken by the schooner Rollo of Baltimore. Her captors were sending her home as a prize. Of this we were not made acquainted until we had got out to sea. When we set sail, we had nine men sick with the yellow fever, six of whom died and were consigned to the vasty deep, after the usual ceremony of the reading of prayers, &c. We were off the east end of Cuba, when we discovered early in the morning, a large sail to the eastward, which we took to be an American man-of-war, but soon found we had been fatally deceived, for she was a large English sloop-of-war called the Sapho, Capt. O'Brady. She fired a broad side which sent all hands below except the captain and mate.— She then stopped firing and run down upon us, and asked us if we did not know it was war time, to which we answered in the affirmative. She then run under our lee, and sent her launch and jolly boat with 30 men, who boarded us. The Capt. having the old license from the British Admiralty with him, presented it to the boarding master, who immediately went on deck and informed the Capt. of the sloop that the schooner had a good license, and was told by the Capt. to overhaul her well, and let her go, if all was right. The boarding master then went below and told the Capt. that he would overhaul his trunk, which he refused, but after some threats from the former, the latter gave up the keys. Search was then made and a commission from the schooner Rollo was found, and the uniform coat of the Captain. This took from us all chance of escape, for immediately after, a prize master and twelve men from the sloop were sent aboard of us to take charge. The Capt. of the English sloop then told the prize master to leave all the American sick board the prize, and

send the others aboard of his vessel. They then ordered all
our crew aboard the sloop except the second mate and myself,
who feigned ourselves sick.

Sometime during the afternoon, the sloop gave chase to an
American privateer, and the prize ship steered away for Jamaica. Soon after this, Mr. Hutchins, the second mate of the
Mary, gave the British a large supply of rum, in which he had
previously put a quantity of laudanum. This, after a little
time, threw them into a lethargic state, as a matter of course.
After they had become quite sleepy, the mate told me that we
must retake the ship that night, and that I must stand by him,
for he had picked me out of the whole crew of the Mary for
that very purpose. I told him that there was so many well
armed men on board, that I thought the proposed adventure
too hazardous, but he said we could easily accomplish it if
we would be bold, as we should have to have to go to Jamaica and probably die there, unless we could free ourselves that
night. I then told him I would stand by him. The sleepy crew
were now all in the steerage, except the the prize master, who
was in the cabin asleep. Eight o'clock in the evening, was
the time agreed upon to commence operations. When that
hour arrived, the mate directed me to go below and seize the
officer in the cabin, while he would secure the hatchway and
prevent the crew from making their way to the deck. All now
depended on doing business with despatch. While hurrying
below, I slipped and fell upon the deck; this waked my an-
tagonist, whom I intended to catch napping, but imagine my
disappointment when he jumped from his berth like a tiger who
had been suddenly awakened by a band of hunters; but I was
ready, and as he struck the deck and was in the act of draw-
ing his sword I closed around him, fastening his arms from behind by grasping him firmly ; but he was a powerful man and
I but a boy, still I was determined and resolute. After squab-
ling for some time, he shook me from him, and while in the act
of turning to face me, I gave him a blow under the chin that
felled him to the deck. I then cut his belt as soon as thought,
and threw his pistols and sword under the cabin steps; just
at this time, Mr. Hutchins, who had succeeded in his part of
the enterprize, threw a hatchet to me and told me to split the
officer's head open if he attempted to get up. This I took and
holding it over his head, told him I would finish him in an in-

stant if he moved. At this juncture Mr. H. came to my assistance, and we soon finished the business by putting the prize
master in irons.

After all this was done we armed ourselves and steered away
for St. Jago, a Spanish port on the Island of Cuba.

My comrade and myself now had full command, and felt
ourselves free. We took turns in watching the crew, and every
thing went on well until the next morning, when our hopes of
freedom were suddenly blighted, even when we were in plain
sight of, and but three miles from, the port to which we were
steering, by being retaken by the same sloop which had taken
us the day before. They immediately put us in irons, which
they kept on us for fifteen days thereafter. Thus we were
doomed to the most cruel disappointment. We were now put
on board the sloop, which sailed for Kingston, on the Island of
Jamaica; but she had sailed but a few days before she gave
chase to an American privateer. A running fight was kept up
between these two war vessels until towards night, when the
British sloop had her main-top-mast shot away. This took
some little time to repair, after which we steered for our place
of destination, where we arrived in about three days. While
making the port we run aground and were not able to get off
until about four o'clock next morning, and then by the aid of a
British man-of-war, which was lying at Port Royal.

The captain of the sloop kindly kept us on board his vessel
for two weeks; after which we were sent on board of a prison
ship, where we remained eight months While here we fared
very poorly, having only half a pound of meat, a pound of bread
and a gill of peas per day. There were nine hundred American prisoners confined in this vessel, shut out from home and
all its many endearments. Many of them were sick with yellow fever, and met here their final exit far from friends and
home.

After the expiration of the above time, six of us got away,
by swimming about a fourth of a mile to a vessel which lay at
anchor in the harbor, the jolly boat of which we made bold
to take into our possession, and steered out of the port through
a great number of men-of-war in safety.

Early the next morning, we captured a small fishing canoe
manned by five slaves, from which we took a turtle, four fish,
a sail and three paddles. Immediately afterwards we heard

the alarm guns fired aboard of the ship from which we had but just made our escape. We then made for shore, drew our boat into a swamp, and lay concealed all of that day. When night came, we drew our boat to the water and pulled away for St. Domingo. The next day we discovered an English Drogger, manned with slaves, seventeen in number, and loaded with porter and cheese. This craft we boarded and took possession of, after putting the slaves aboard of our craft and giving them a small part of the loading of the vessel. We then steered away for New Orleans, but ill luck again attended us, for we had not had possession of her but a few hours before an English man-of-war gave chase to, and compelled us to run ashore to save being retaken. But we had not been on shore long before we were again taken by some soldiers and marched about thirty miles back into the country, and lodged in a stone jail, where we remained 25 days. Then we were marched down to the sea shore and put aboard the Sea-Horse frigate, and carried back to Port Royal, where we were put in irons and again placed on board the prison ship. Thus were all our hopes of freedom again destroyed, when we thought our liberty was almost within our grasp. After this we were kept on half the usual quantity of provisions for about a month, to pay us for our love of liberty and fresh air, and hard pay we thought it was too.

We were again put in irons and otherwise harshly treated, and had given up all hope of ever seeing our native shores, when one day soon after this, Captain Joseph Merryhew, from Wilmington, in Delaware, was brought on board the prison ship with nine other prisoners. This man knew, and inquired of me how long I had been a prisoner. I told him, and he promised to help me to obtain my freedom; which promise he faithfully kept. He was a freemason, and a kind hearted man; and to his influence I own my early release from the miseries of imprisonment, which I had borne for nearly a year. This humane man procured not only my release but a large number more of my poor countrymen. This was a happy change to men who were sighing for freedom.

We hoisted sail sometime in the month of August, 1814, and steered away for Baltimore. Our ship was called the William Penn. Captain Turner. In about eighteen days after leaving Port Royal, we made Cape Henry, on the Virginia coast, where we found a British blockading fleet at anchor, the commander of which ordered us to Philadelphia, to which port we steered away, but we had the bad luck to strike upon the shoals of Barnegat, during a thick fog that came on that afternoon, but after three hours hard labor we got off and went on our voyage and soon made the Delaware bay, which was also blockaded. Here we were again refused the privilege of going into port, but were ordered to Boston, and were told by the British officers to get out to sea within three hours or they would fire into us. At this time we were almost out of provisions and water. Of this we made the tyrant officers acquainted, but they utterly refused either to furnish us with these necessaries or permit us to enter Philadelphia. So we were again compelled to go to sea with one day's provisions and water, and steered away for Boston. The next day about 10 o'clock, A. M., we made Great Egg Harbor. The crew then told the Captain that he must go ashore, for they would not stay aboard and starve.— He said he dared not do it. They then told him that they would give him half an hour to think of it, and if he did not then comply that they should take the ship ashore. He however complied, and we steered away accordingly. We were soon aground and were compelled to throw overboard all the ballast, casks, and every thing on board; however, after much hard struggling with the sand and waves we got over the bar, and got as near shore as possible, where we drove stubs down to keep the vessel. After which, we stripped her of all her rigging and sails. The next morning we saw the shore lined with the militia of New Jersey, who took us to be an enemy, but they soon found their mistake. Instead of an enemy, they found us a poor set of weather-beaten, starved fellows. Soon after this, the Custom-House officer sent down boats and took us off, and carried us to the village that was near by, and gave us all a good dinner; after which, we dispersed; some went to New-York, and some to Philadelphia. This was about the middle of September, 1814. Two hundred and seven of the crew started the next day after we got ashore, for Philadelphia by land, which was about one hundred and fifty miles. With this number I journied. We suffered much on our journey, being destitute of money, and being compelled to beg what little we eat on the road. At night we slept in the woods. We were seven days in getting to the place of our destination, two of which we eat nothing but whortleberries, which we picked by the way side. On the third day a Friend Quaker kindly provided us with a good breakfast and gave us money to pay our bridge fare. This man's name was John Rogers ; and of him it may be truly said, " he did unto others as he would have them do unto him." How few of the pious of this covetous age can be found to exhibit as much real disinterested benevolence as this man did. After this we did not suffer for want of food.

We arrived at Philadelphia, and from thence we went either to sea or to our several homes. After getting my pay, I went again to see my parents at Westport. Here I stayed until spring, when I again shipped aboard the ship Traveller. Jonathan Kendricks, master. The crew numbered seventeen souls, principally Cape Cod men.. We sailed for the Straits of Belisie, where we went after codfish. We sailed as far north as Esquimaux bay, where we took in one hundred and sixty thousand fish in the short space of forty-five days. We then sailed for Boston. When off Nantucket we experienced a severe gale, which continued all one night, during which time the ship struck on the shoals ; but after two hours we got off and put into Chatham, on Cape Cod. We lost our main-mast during this gale, and all the boats but one ; besides this, we lost one man by the name of Hagars, who fell from the fore-top and was drowned. We dried our fish at Chatham and refitted before sailing for Boston, at which place we arrived some time in December. He we disposed of our fish and returned to New Bedford and stayed until spring.

The next trip which I made to sea, was in the brig America, of 200 tons, William Dagget, master. We sailed from Boston with a crew of ten men, and twenty-five passengers, on a cruise to New Orleans, which we made in twenty days.

While opposite Cape Florida, we fell in with a pirate schooner, which gave chase to us by coming down upon our larboard quarter, and giving us a gun which passed through our bulwark. Our Captain at this juncture advised a surrender of our vessel, but the mate declared he would not give up if the men would stand by him. The passengers told him they would fight as long as there was a man left. They then stripped off their coats, and we cleared for action. We then fired a broad side, which cut away the pirate's main-mast and killed several of hei crew. We fired several broad-sides, and the passengers fired the small aims to good effect, for the enemy soon wore away to windward and got off as soon as possible by means of their oars. We saw several dead bodies floating on the water belonging to the pirate crew. We had but one man wounded and none killed.

We stayed at New Orleans three weeks, took in a load of Cotton, and again sailed for Providence, where we arrived after a passage of thirty days. Here we discharged our cargo and took in a set of ballast, and after staying about twenty days we again set sail for Richmond, in Virginia, after flour. We took in 1700 barrels of flour at the latter place and after staying about three weeks again set sail for Boston, where we arrived after a sail of fifteen days. Here we were paid off and discharged; after which I went home to New Bedford, my parents at this time being dead. Here I stayed until the next June. 1817, when I shipped aboard of the Alexander Barclay, Captain Joseph Dunbar, bound to Baltimore, for Cotton, Fustick, and Tobacco-stalks. After loading our vessel with the above articles, we set sail for Bremen, a town in Germany, on the river Weser. We had three passengers, Dr. Jamison, wife and daughter. We were four weeks in loading our vessel and thirty days on our passage to Bremen. We had an excellent Captain. At Bremen we stayed but three weeks, discharged our freight. took in ballast, and two passengers, a Swedish lady and her daughter. From here we sailed to Gottenburgh, which took us fifteen days. Here we took in a load of lion, stayed four weeks, and again set sail for New Bedford, which place we reached in forty-seven days thereafter. We went north about between Scotland and the Ferroe Islands — When on the banks. we saw large islands of ice which contained a number of hundred acres, and some of them one hundred and fifty feet high. We arrived at New Bedford about the first of January, 1818. The next year I spent principally around home. But in May 1819, I shipped aboard of the brig Traveller again, on a cruise to Cape Harrison, in latitude 65 degrees north, where we took in twelve hundred quintals of codfish. While here we killed four white bears. Wild geese were very plenty. We saw the Esquimaux Indians a number of times sailing in their skin canoes. We made this voyage in about six months. We sold our fish at Boston, and went home to Bedford, where all hands were paid off and discharged.

The next voyage that I made was with Captain Joseph Gardner, to Matanzas, in the ship William, for Molasses, Coffee, and Sugar. This was in the year 1820. The seas were thickly infested with pirates at this time, which detained us eighteen days after we were loaded. Captain Porter at this time lay off Matanzas, in the sloop Peacock. He had a number of schooners also under his command, two of which convoyed us with sixty other merchantmen across the Bahama banks.

The next fall I went another voyage in the Mary, of Boston, Captain Joseph White, to St. Thomas for Molasses, which we carried to Boston.

During the next eight years I made sixteen voyages to the West India Islands, under different Captains and in different vessels. In none of these voyages did any thing unusual occur, though we had to throw some of our cargoes overboard to save the vessels. After the above voyages I stayed at home a few months, but not being contented on shore, about the 25th of June, 1829, I again went to sea in the ship Trident, of 600 tons. There were sixty of the crew, principally experienced whalemen. We were bound to the Pacific Ocean, for whale. Our course was as usual by way of the Western Islands, where we arrived in about 20 days. We caught three Sperm on the passage. We stopped Flores, one of these islands, where we took in potatoes, onions, pumpkins, hogs, and chickens. Here we stopped but two days. Then we steered away south for the Cape De Verds, which we passed. The next land which we saw was the Isle of May. Thence we steered away for Cape Horn, where we arrived in 90 days thereafter. We then doubled Cape Horn, and sailed northward off the coast, until we came to the island of Juan Fernandez, famous for its being for several years the abode of the celebrated Robinson Crusoe. One could not help thinking of the dreadful life this celebrated navigator lived while here. His lonely hours and tantalizing dreams. His constant fear of beasts and cannibal savages. While here we visited the untenanted cave where that noted adventurer is said to have resided. On this island are a great many goats; also peaches, which grow wild in the woods. There were but few people here. The colony planted by Crusoe not having multiplied very fast. The land here

is good, but the shore is generally bold. From this place we
sailed for Payta, in latitude 5 degrees south, where we arrived
after more than six months sail from the time we left New
Bedford. Here we took in potatoes and onions, re-fitted ship,
and made ready for fishing. Here we stayed eighteen days.
Then we sailed for the "off shore ground," a famous place for
sperm whale. We were fifty days sailing from Payta to the
shore. Here we stayed five months. and took but two hundred barrels sperm. We then sailed again for Payta, where
we recruited ship, staid a couple of weeks, and then sailed
for Tombus, where we took in wood and water. When this
was done, we sailed the for Gallipago Islands, where we went
for Terrapin. The Terrapin very much resembles our large
Turtle, only they live wholly on the land, and weigh from four
to five hundred pounds. The manner of taking them is as fol-
lows : In the morning we used to go up into the island, among
the bushes, where we usually found them feeding upon cab-
bage trees, that they had gnawed down the night before. After finding them two of us used to go up to them and turn them
over upon their backs, then tie their legs, and swing them between us, by lashing them to our backs. We then carry them
to the boats, and from thence to the ship. We sometimes keep
them alive six months without any food or drink. They make
excellent soup, and are esteemed very healthy. They are
worth, when brought to a sea-port city, from two hundred to
three hundred dollars. We took six hundred of these animals
in five days, and got them on board ship.
     After this, we went again to the "off shore" coast, for sperm
whale. We had the luck to take six whale after we had been
out two days. After this we continued our sail to the place of
destination, where we took in eighteen hundred barrels of oil.
Here we stayed three months, and sailed for Callao, on the
coast of Peru. After arriving at the latter place, I left the ship
and went aboard of the Charles, of London. The Trident,
after recruiting ship sailed for New Bedford.
     The Charles, on board of which I had shipped, sailed in
about two weeks after I went aboard, for sperm, along the
coast, but we had such a drunken Captain that we could not
do any business. He was not sober any of the time while we
were out. After going into the port from whence we last sailed, I left the Charles and went on board the Golconda, of New

Bedford. In this vessel I stayed about nine months, during which we fished in Panamà bay with tolerable success. The Captain was a bad man and abused the crew very much.— From this bay we went to Payta, where I was paid off and left the ship.

The people of this place procure their water from springs that are nine miles off, which is brought in every morning on asses in what are called callabashes, that hold from fifteen to twenty gallons each. After staying at this place five months, myself and two others started with one ass loaded with water and provisions for Peuro, situated one hundred miles south east from Payta. The country through which we passed was a sandy desert, without a shrub or spire of grass to cheer us on our way. At night we slept on the sand and had no other shelter than the canopy of the heavens afforded. We were five days on our journey. There was no water to be seen during our whole journey, nor a single house or cultivated spot. The sands drift as the snow does in the northern parts of America. When I arrived at the place of our destination, I engaged to work for Spanish gentleman called Don Francisco. This man owned a distillery in which I labored two months. Then I went about 70 miles further into the country, to a place called Apputaria, which was situated on the Columbian mountains. Here I labored five months on a farm, for a man named Tarbury. The people in this vicinity are Spaniards, and are very hospitable to strangers. Here the people live by raising sweet potatoes, corn, cotton and sugar cane. Here I stayed six months and enjoyed myself very well. The religion of this people is the Catholic.

The only man with whom I had formed an acquaintance who was from the United States, was a Cape-Cod man. This man and myself had lived together from the time I landed at Payta. From Apputaria we started about the first of March, 1834, and went again to Peuro, where my companion died, far from home and friends, in a foreign land. He had no kind friend to close his eyes for the last time, except the writer of this narrative, who rendered him such assistance as was in his power to render, and when he slept in death, procured him such a burial as was in accordance with the custom of the country.

After the death of my friend I stayed about a week, and then left that place and went to Payta, which is a sea-port town.—

c

Here I stayed but about one month before I again shipped on board a whaler called the Mechanic, of Newport, Rhode Island. After leaving this port we went down to Tombus, where we took in potatoes, squashes, onions and water melons. We then steered away for the off shore ground, which is about three thousand miles west of the coast of Peru. Here we took two whale, after which we steered away west until we came to the Reupore Islands, but we did not land here on account of the ferocity of the natives, who were armed with heavy, carved war-clubs. The land appeared to be good, but was mountainous, back from the shore. The people were almost white, but very savage in their appearance, and went almost naked.— What little clothing they had was made of grass wove into a species of cloth. This they tied around their waists. It reached down before nearly to the knees. These people have never permitted the missionaries to live among them, but they worship idols made of stone. They raise potatoes and oranges of the vegetable kind, and of the animal, hogs. Of these latter, we purchased a hog that would weigh two hundred pounds, for one whale tooth. What they do with the teeth I do not know. This the natives brought to us by swimming to the ship. From the last mentioned Islands we steered away west by north, about two thousand miles further, when we reached an island called Riotier, one of a group called the Society Islands. Here my time being up, I left the ship and went among the natives, who were a very friendly, hospitable people. Here I stayed five months, and learned much of the customs and manners of the country. The people generally go naked, and men, women and children live promiscuously together.

Their houses are very simple, being constructed by driving posts into the ground and then by fastening beams made of round sticks to the top of these posts, and smaller sticks, covered with grass wove very compactly together to the beams. This forms the dwelling of these poor, but happy people. When the wind blows hard, or when it rains they heave up grass mats on the side of the house towards the wind. Under this frail covering whole families, sometimes consisting of twenty or thirty, are huddled together both by night and by day. The people are very indolent, having every thing necessary for their subsistence growing spontaneously around them. Their food is bread fruit, which grows upon trees somewhat resembling apple trees. It grows like an apple, but as large as a man's head. This is prepared for eating by roasting it in the fire and by taking off the skin. Then it is sliced up the same as we slice up bread for the table. This is better than the best wheat bread. Of this fruit they have two crops in a year which lasts about two months and a half each crop. Then they have during the other parts of year two crops of Fayees, a kind of fruit that grows upon bushes about ten feet high and resembles large cucumbers. These are cooked by digging holes in the ground and then making hot fires in them and heating the same as we heat ovens. When the hole is sufficiently hot they clear out the fire, put in the fruit, and cover them over with large leaves. In about two hours they are sufficiently cooked.— When cooked, they become soft like a potatoe, but much more delicious. There is also a root, called tea-root, which is about four inches in diameter and two or three feet long.— These, when roasted, afford a juice similar to molasses. Besides these, they have plenty of good fish, hogs and cattle. Horses are very scarce, though I saw a few while there.

The people of this place, when they make a feast, which is often, roast a hog whole. This they do by digging a hole in the ground sufficiently large to put the animal in, then they build a large fire in it and heat it. as English people heat their ovens. While they are making the dirt oven ready, they have another large fire close by, where they heat small round stones. When these are sufficiently heated and the hole is also heated, they clear out the coals, and put a layer of the heated round stones upon the bottom, then they lay in the hog and cover it with large leaves, then over these a layer of the hot stones, then another of the leaves, and over all, they throw a layer of dirt. When the hog has become properly roasted, they take it out and lay it upon sticks prepared for that purpose, and the guests set round and eat.

There is an Englishman by the name of Hunter, who has a sugar plantation on this island, and employs seventy five hands, all natives of the country. He has about one hundred and seventy five acres under improvement. The sugar manufactured here is of good quality. There is a kind of root grows here called tarrow, which resembles a potatoe. This is the only vegetable that I saw cultivated on the island. To raise these, the people burn over a spot during the dry season, and sow the

seed, and get it in with sticks, where the land is not very mel-
low. It generally will sprout, and grow without any labor being
bestowed upon it after sowing. The roots are fit for use in three
months. These are cooked by roasting as we roast potatoes.

There is a missionary on this island, and the people are more
intelligent than most of the other islanders in that vicinity.—
They are one of the most peaceable and happy people with
whom the writer was ever acquainted. They seem to be pe-
culiarly the favorites of our Great Father. Possessing one of
the most salubrious of climates, with every thing formed in na-
ture, and growing spontaneously for their support, they are
well fitted to enjoy life and all its attendant blessings. They
are happy in their poverty. and contented. in their simplicity ,
and I assure my readers, that it was not without many painful
sensations, that I left this ocean isle, and its peaceful inhabit-
ants. May God ever be with, and preserve them for their many acts of benevolence, shown to the writer of this narrative,
when a stranger thrown among them, and more than fourteen
thousand miles from the land of his nativity.

One day, after I had been on the island about five months,
I accidentally found a ship at the harbor which belonged to
Martha's Vineyard, in the United States. This was the first
vessel which I had seen since I had been here. The Captain's
name was Toby. After getting acquainted with this man, he
proposed my going home with him. He said I had not better
stay among the natives any longer—that my folks at home
would be glad to see me, I finally concluded to go with him.

We sailed from this place sometime during the latter part of
1835, and arrived at the vineyard in the spring of 1836.

While on our homeward bound passage, we lost three men,
by being struck by a whale.

After discharging our freight at Oldtown, on the Vineyard, I
went home to New Bedford, where I stayed three months,
when I again shipped aboard of a whaler called the Delight,
Captain Philip Sanford. Our voyage was made to St. Domingo in twenty eight days. Here we commenced fishing, but
catched nothing but black fish, which we sold for potatoes,
oranges, squashes &c. We then went down upon the Jamaica
coast, where we caught seven sperm whale ; after this we
went into Mexico Bay where we took four more whale.—
Then we went to the Western Islands, where we caught three

more large whale. We then stopped at Flores, and took in potatoes, onions, chickens, pumpkins and squashes. We stopped at several other of this group of Islands on our way home. We were gone eight months on this voyage. After unloading our ship, I stayed at New Bedford but a few weeks before I again left home on a visit to the State of New York, to see a cousin that I had not seen for more than eighteen years. This man lives in the town of Stockbridge, and county of Madison. His name is Michael Wainer, a man of good property and of respectable standing. I stayed at this place until the spring of 1838, when I went to Buffalo, and shipped aboard of the Steamer Wisconsin, bound to Detroit, in the State of Michigan. We had two hundred and fifty passengers, with their goods, on board. The next trip that we made was to Chicago, in the State of Illinois; our lading was the same as we had in our last trip. On our return passage, I hurt my foot while taking in wood, at Cleaveland in Ohio. After this I boarded a few days in Buffalo, but my foot continuing lame, I again returned to Stockbridge, where I arrived sometime in the month of June, 1838. Here I labored for several persons in the course of the season. I think the people of this place are as industrious and respectable as in any place with which I have been acquainted. They are, in general, good livers, have fewer poor people among them, than most of the places which I have visited, and are very civil and courteous to strangers. They are principally emigrants from the New England States. The town is beautifully situated, having the Oneida Creek, running from south to north through its centre. Upon this stream are a number of grist and saw mills. Here would be an excellent place for erecting manufactories of cotton or wool. From the centre of this town to the Utica and Syracuse Rail Road is but seven miles. This town produces excellent winter wheat, corn, rye, barley and oats. It is called one of the richest towns in the State of New-York.

I now take leave of those who may hereafter peruse this relation of events through which the writer has passed, during his stay among earth's travellers. May heaven's choicest blessings ever be theirs, together with the innumerable comforts which are the attendants of an earthly pilgrimage. Good bye.

PAUL CUFFE.

Stockbridge, N. Y. March 18, 1839.